the Day Dreamer

Izzy Spears

Published by PaSH Publishing

Published in the United States by PaSH Publishing,
an imprint of The Southern PaSH Company.
www.SouthernPash.com

PaSH Publishing and its logo are owned
 by The Southern PaSH Company.

For information about special discounts for bulk
purchases please contact The Southern PaSH
Company by email at southernpashmag@gmail.com

Layout and cover design by Izzy Spears

ISBN 978-0-9992852-3-7

Printed in the United States of America

First Edition

Enjoy today because tomorrow is not promised.
While you are here, create something beautiful.
Izzy

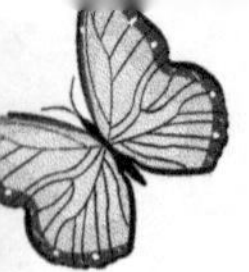

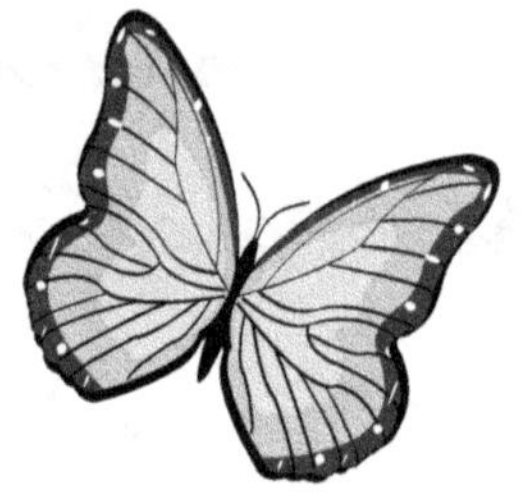

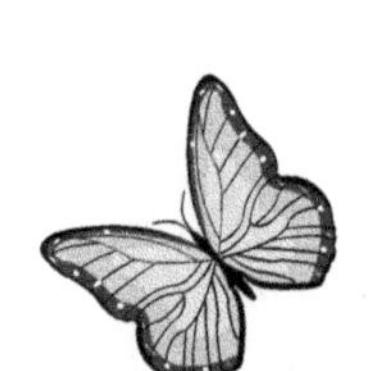
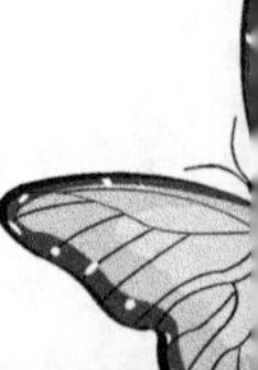

royalty

Queen

throne

I am a

Queen

Queen

throne

royalty

Queen

royalty

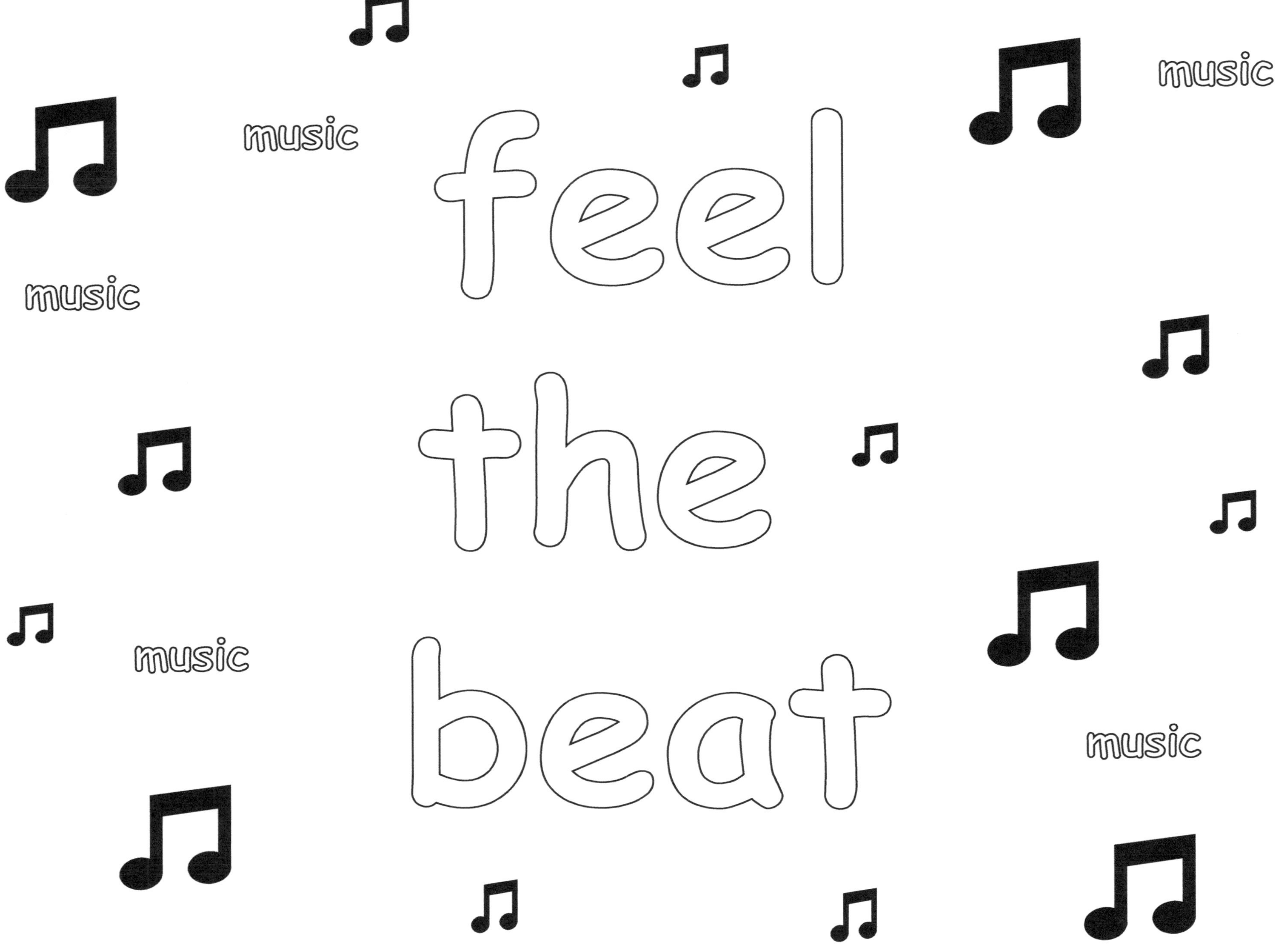

feel
the
beat
music
music
music
music

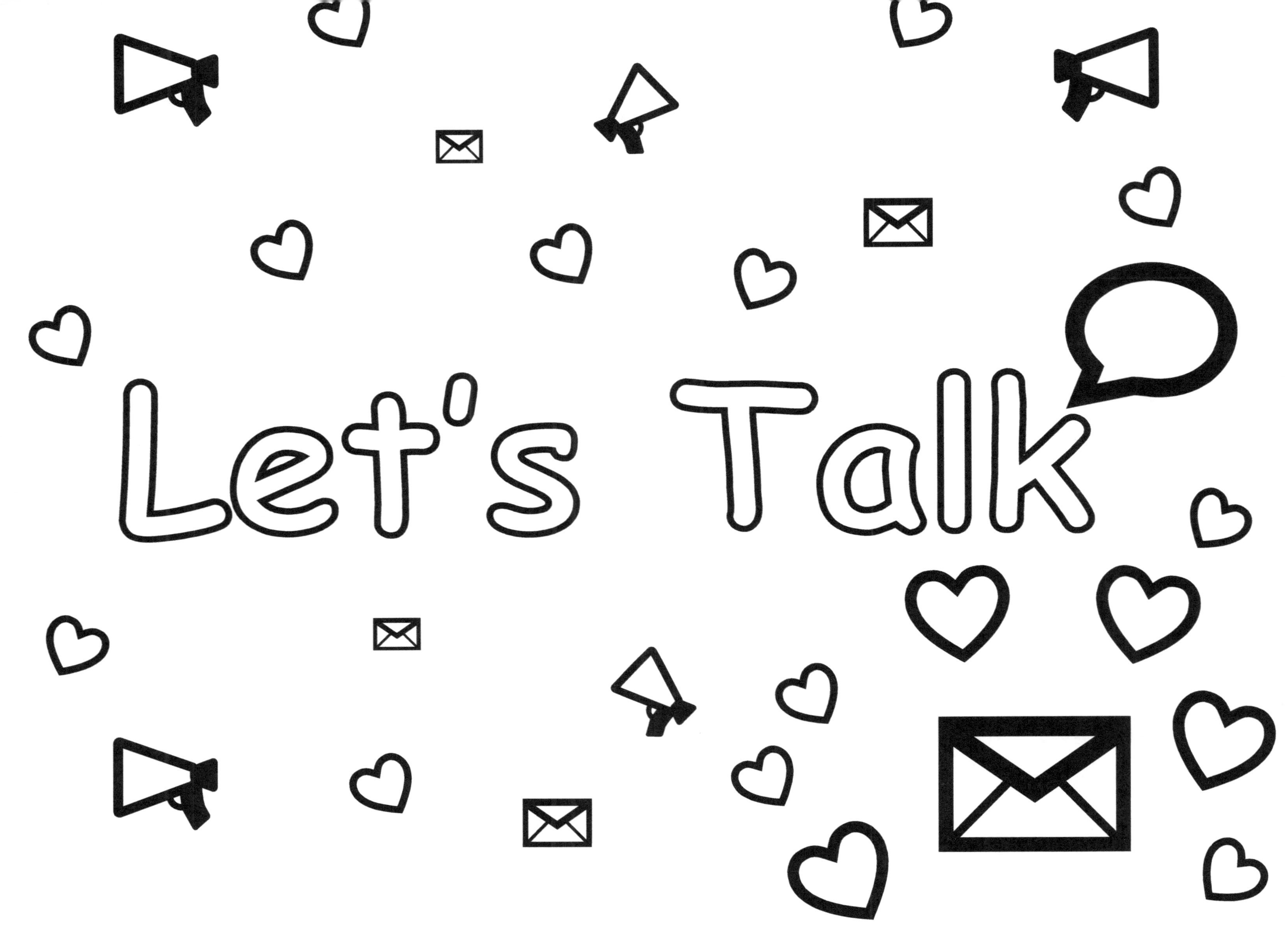

Let's Talk

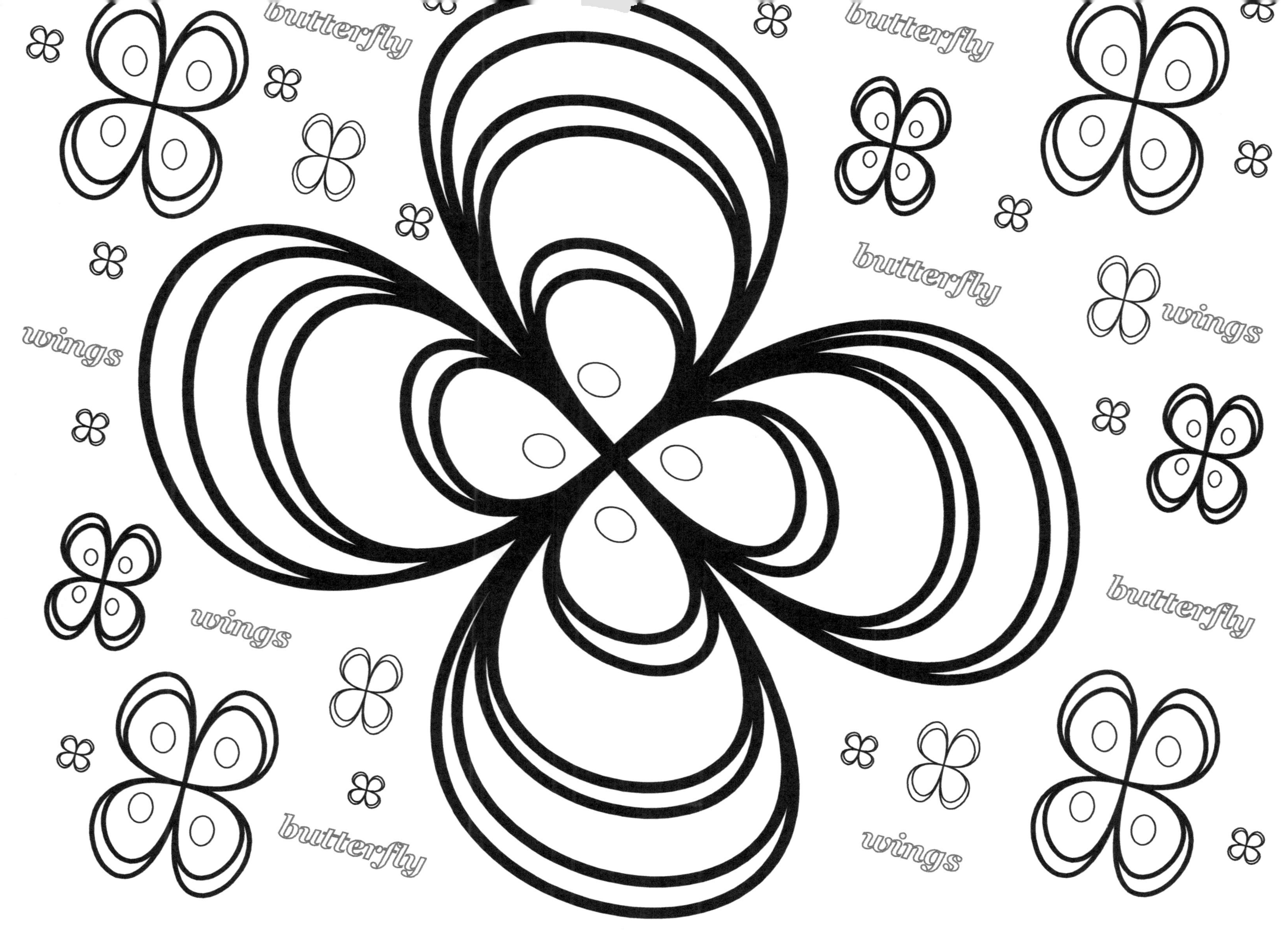

butterfly
wings

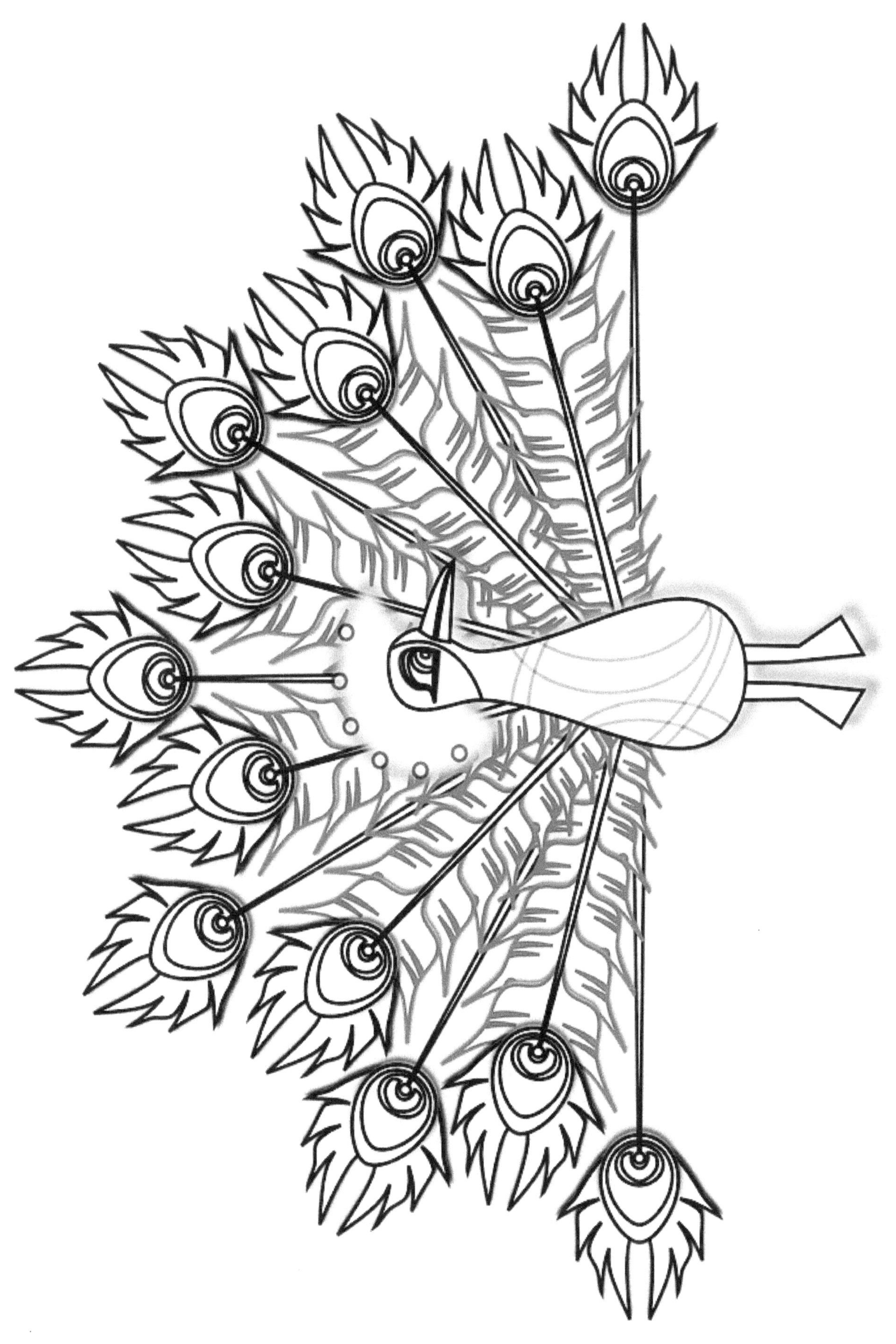

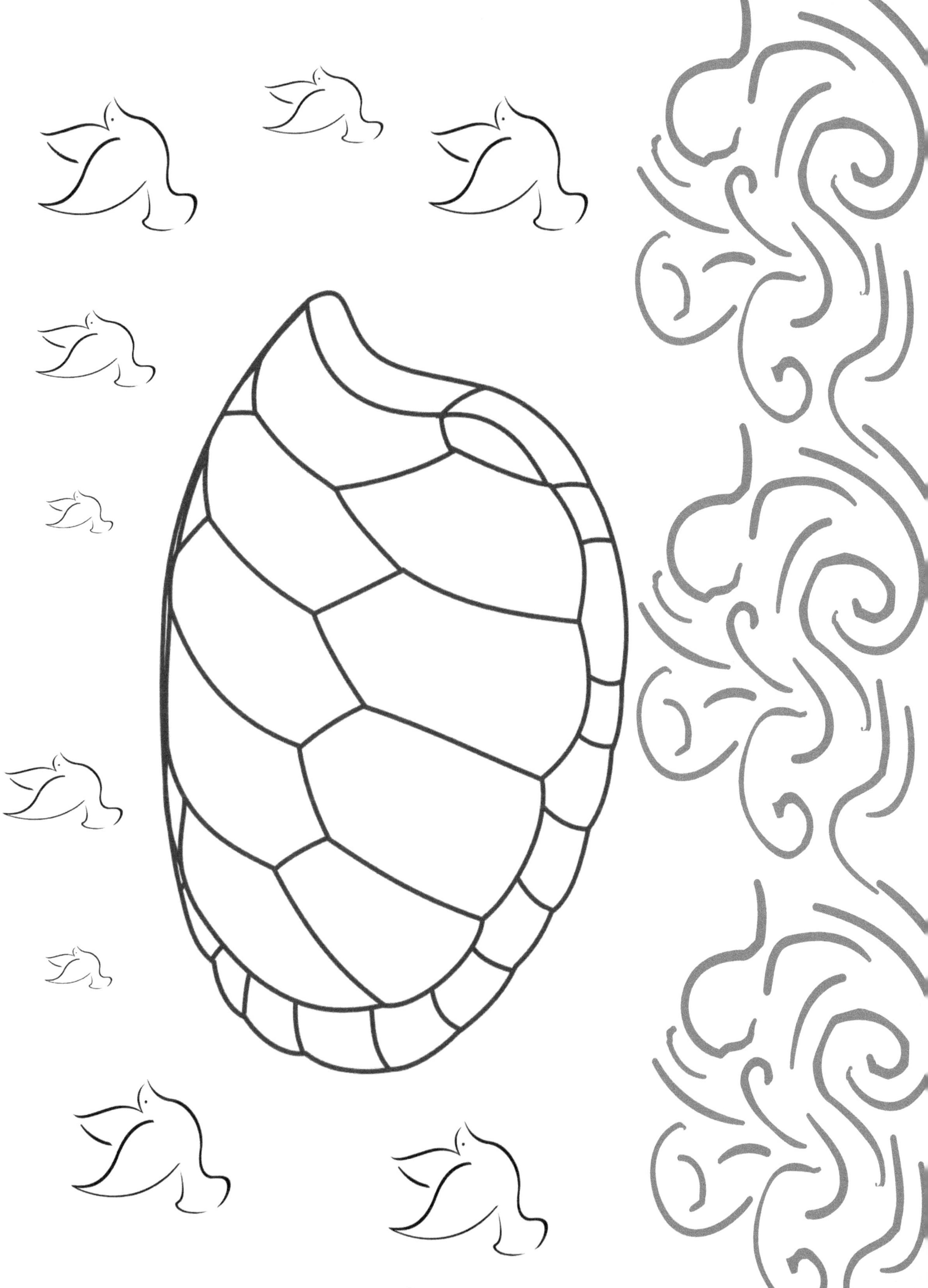

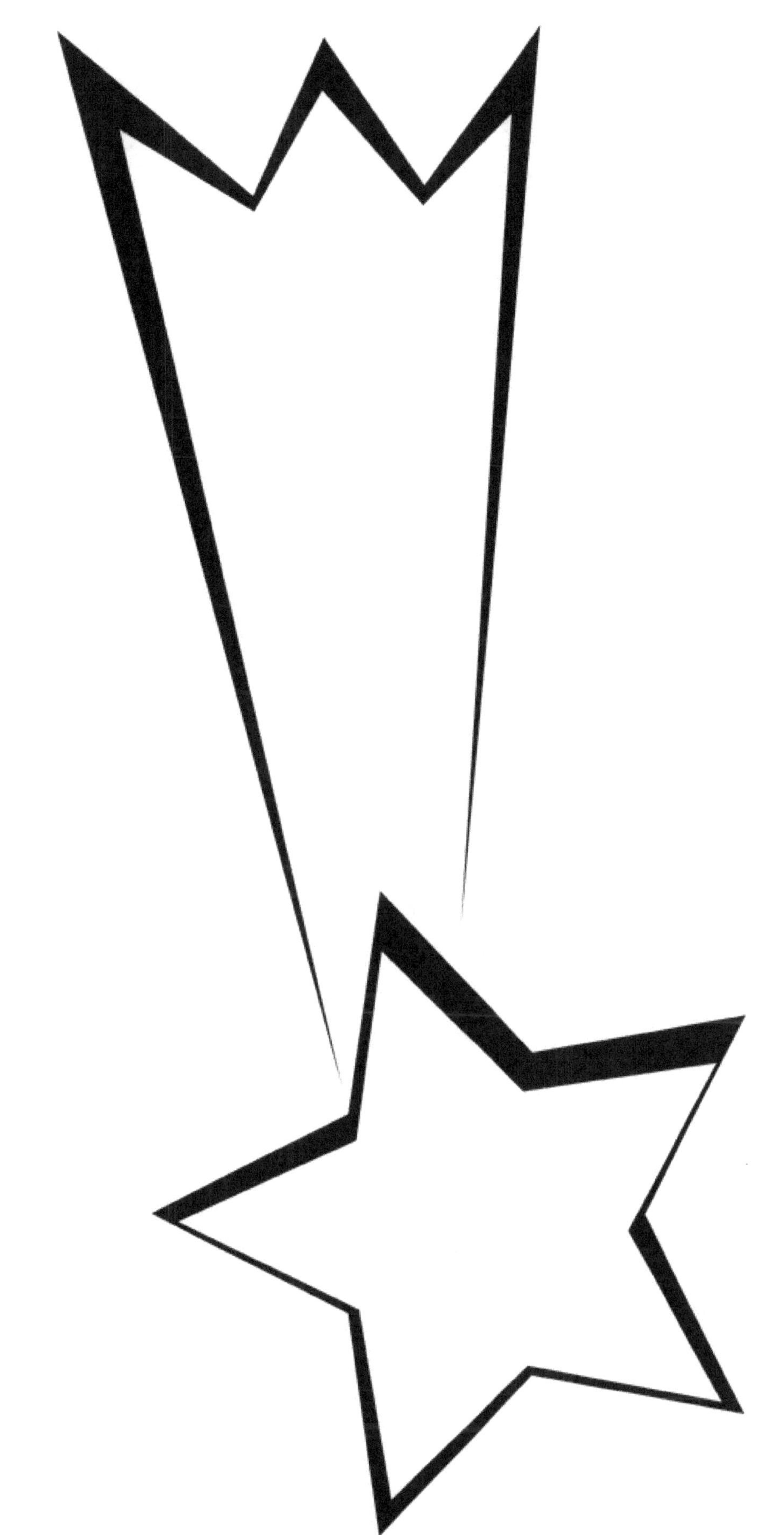

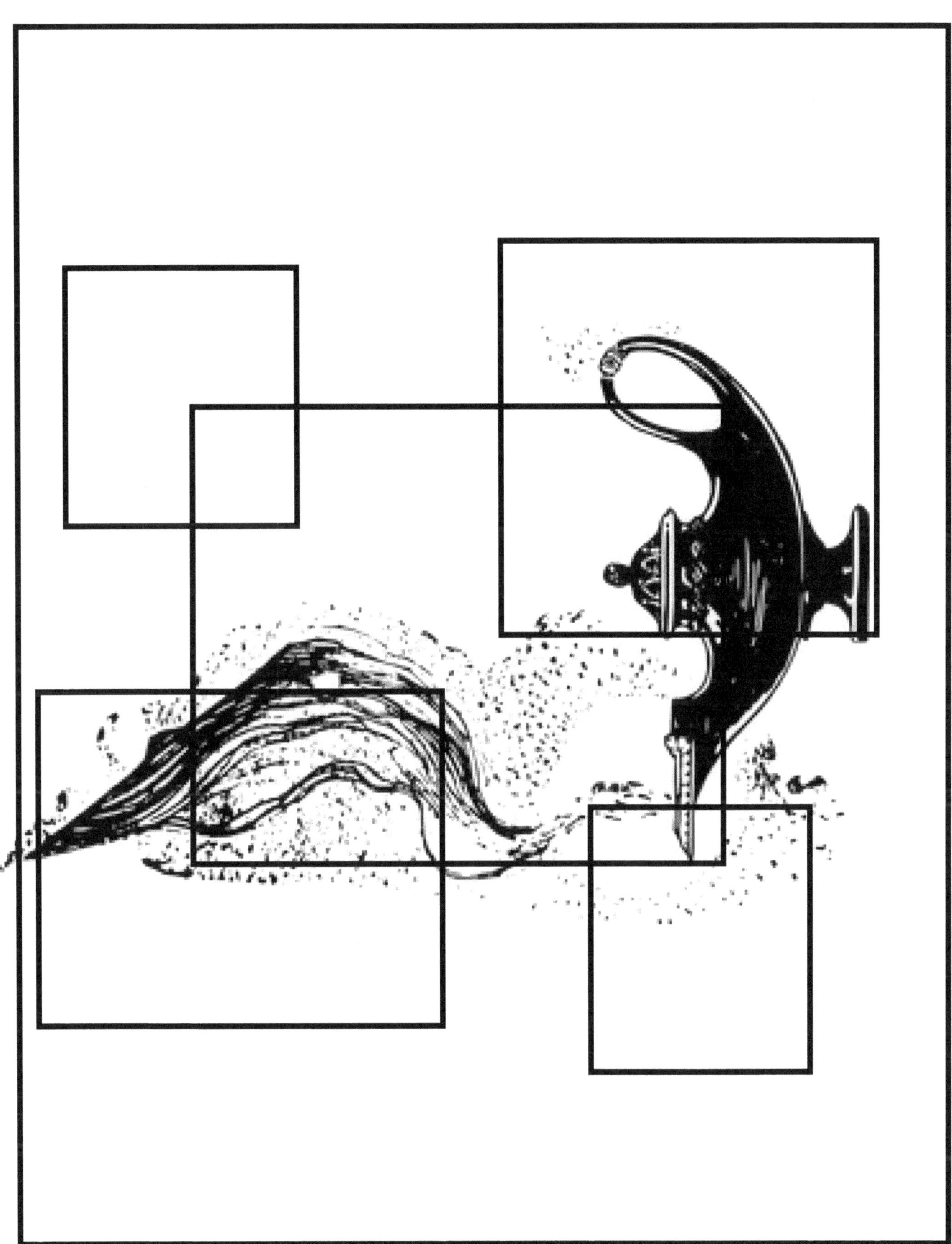

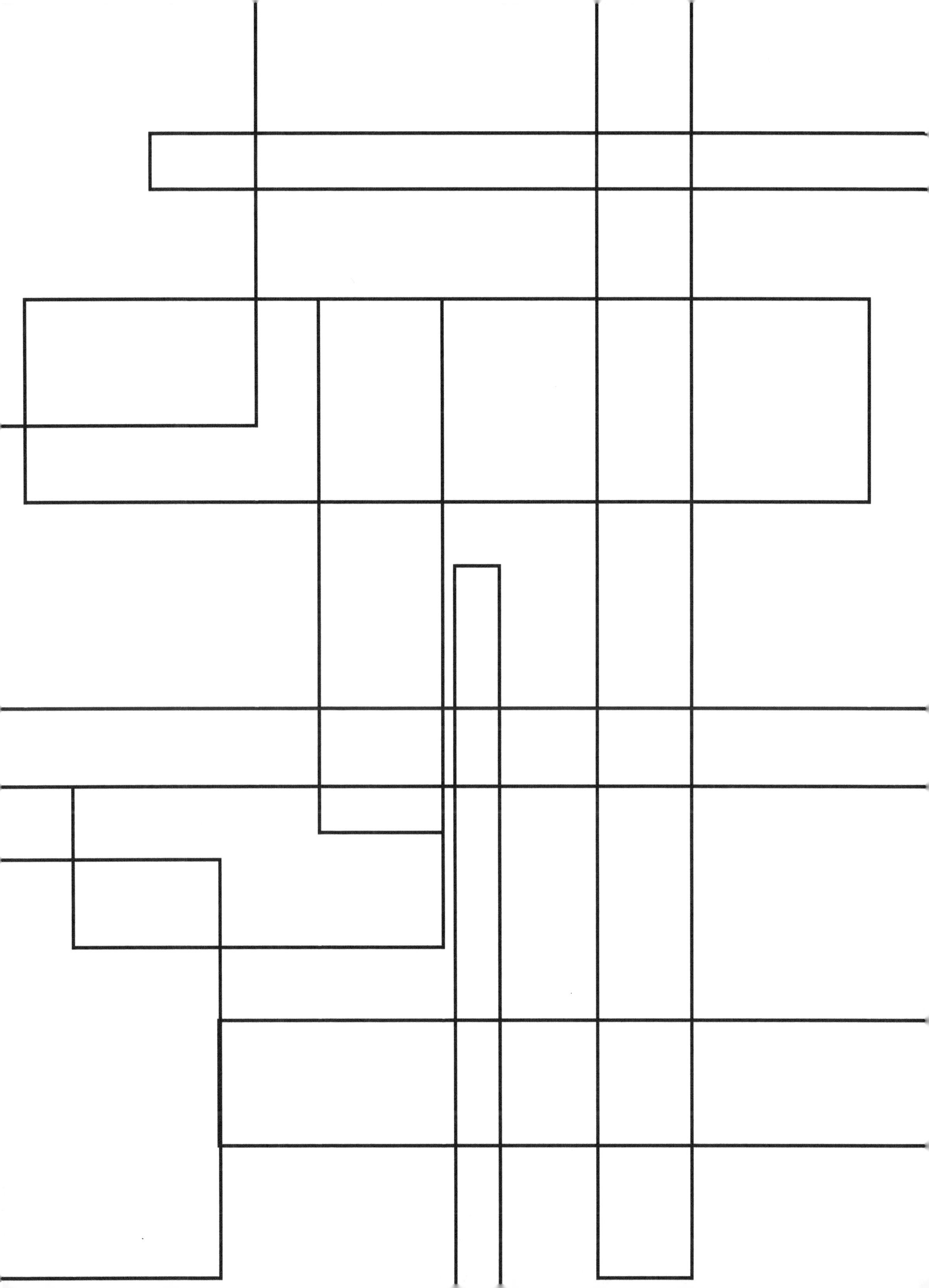

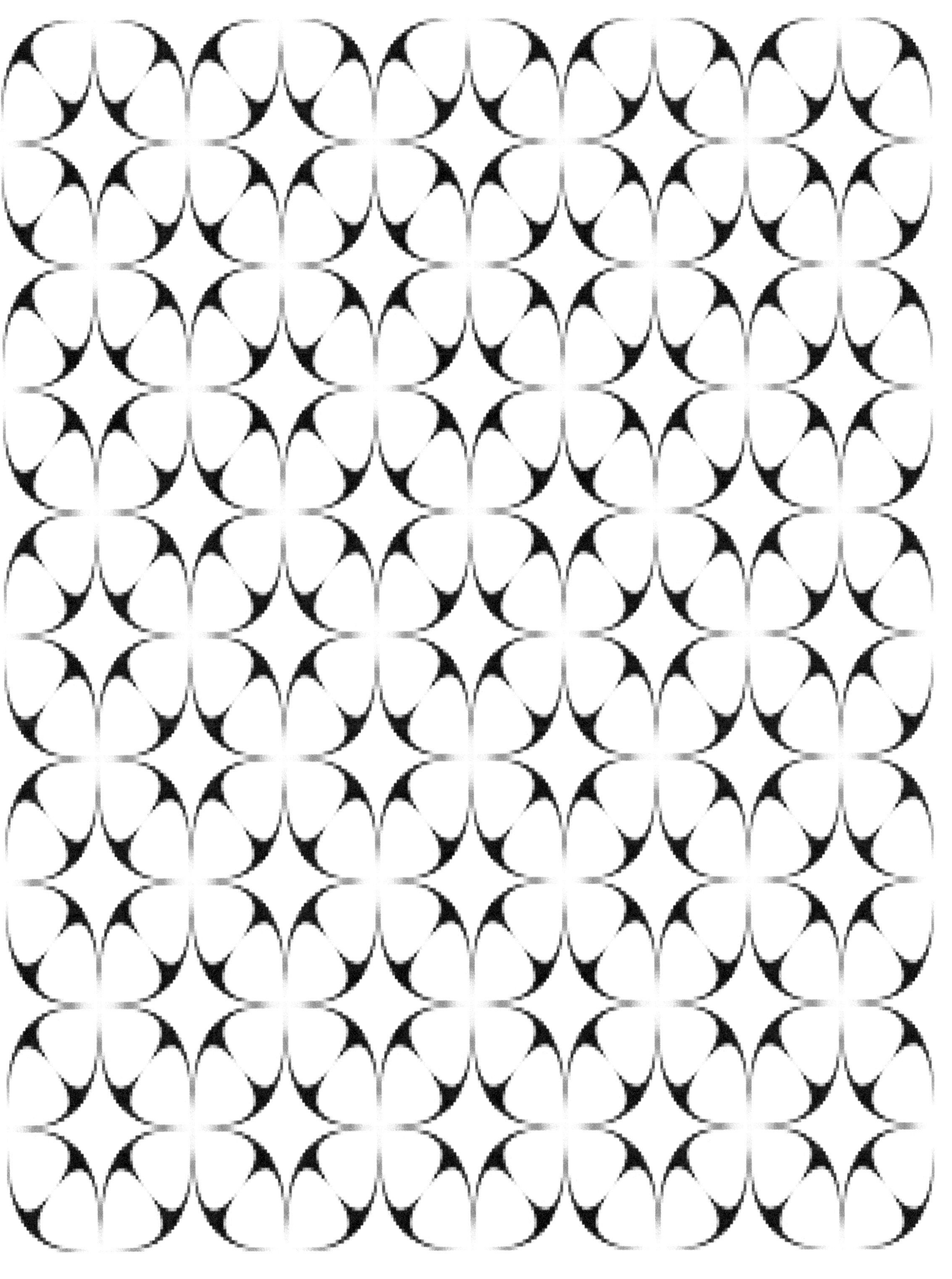

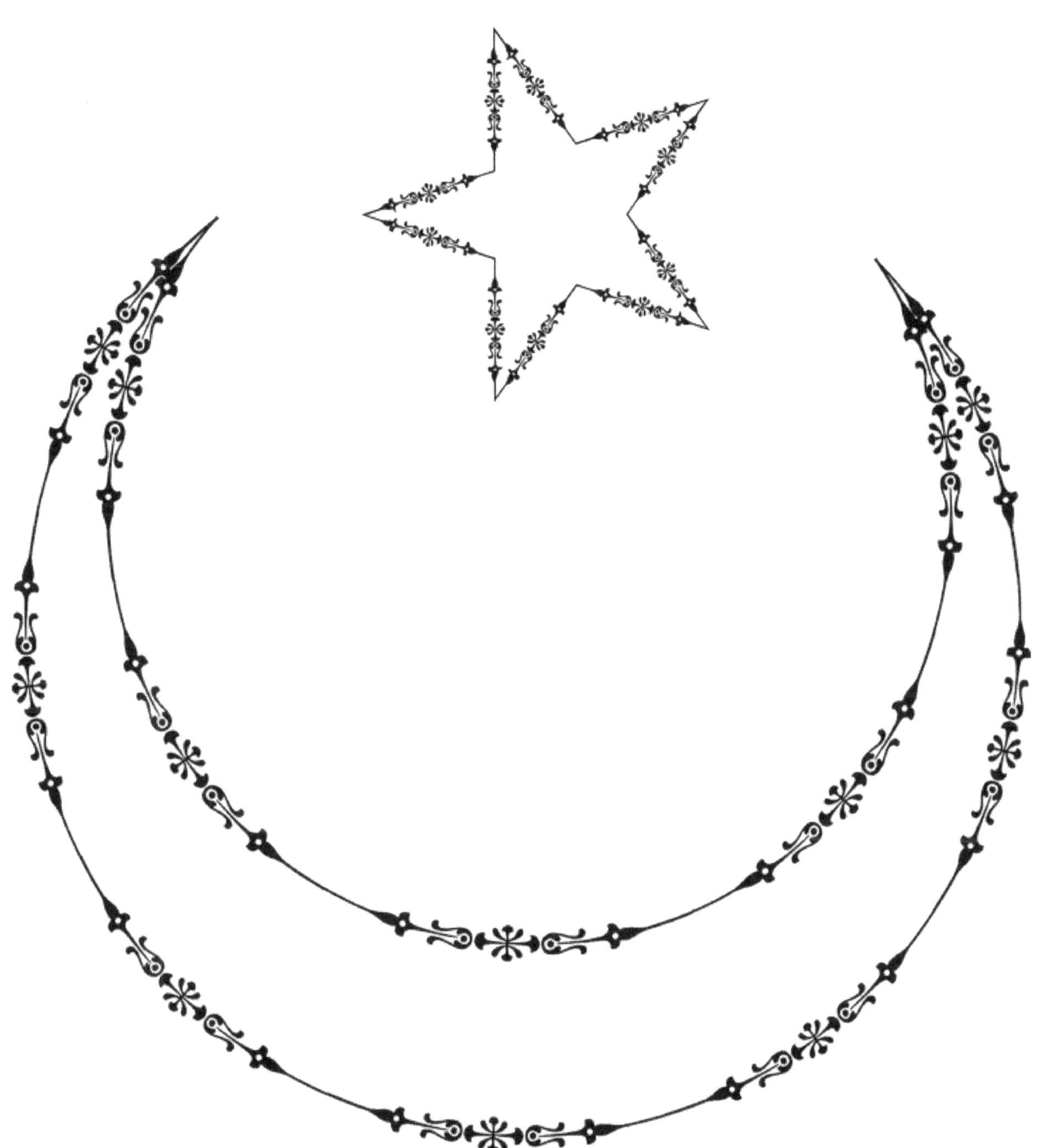

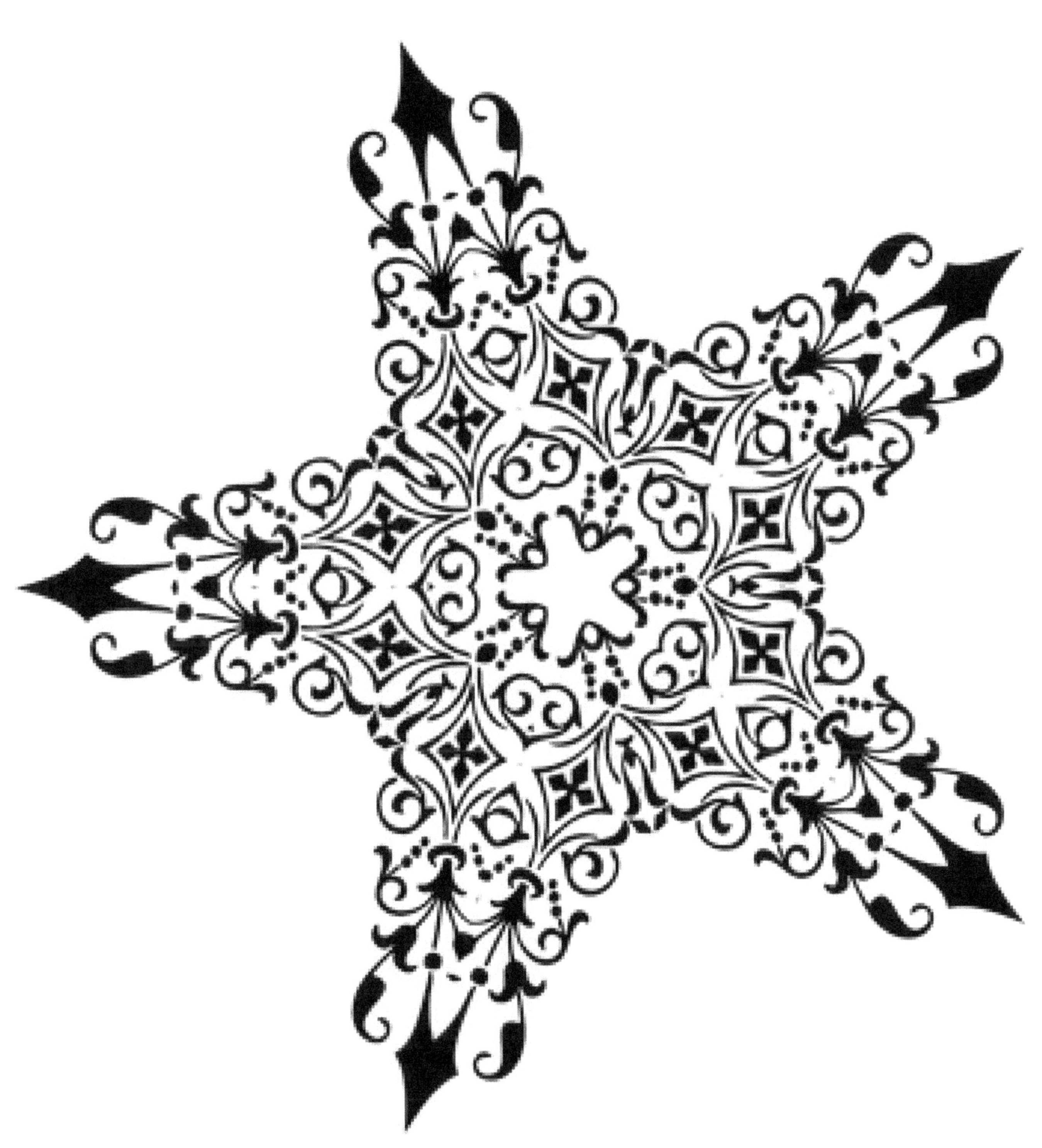

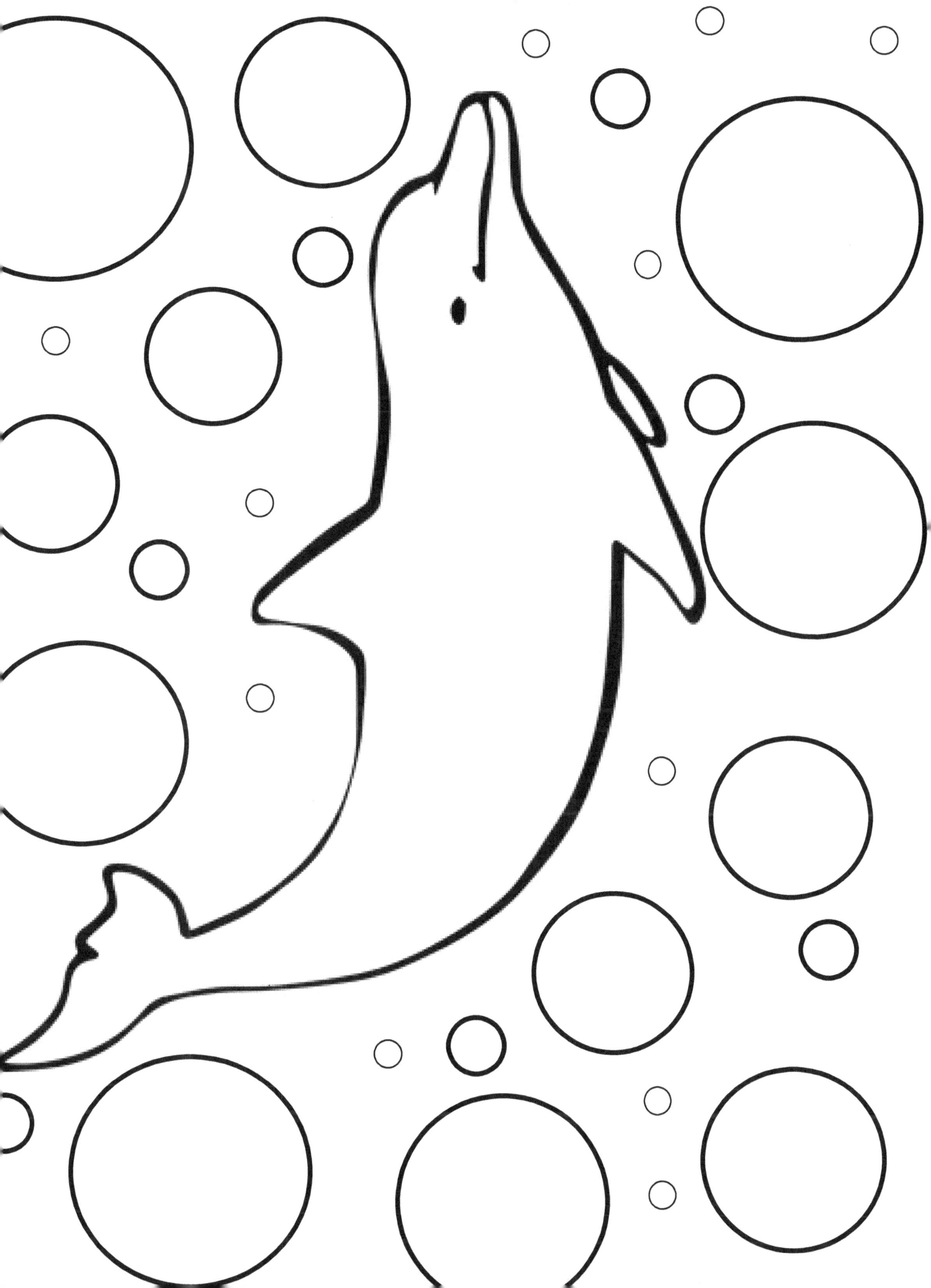

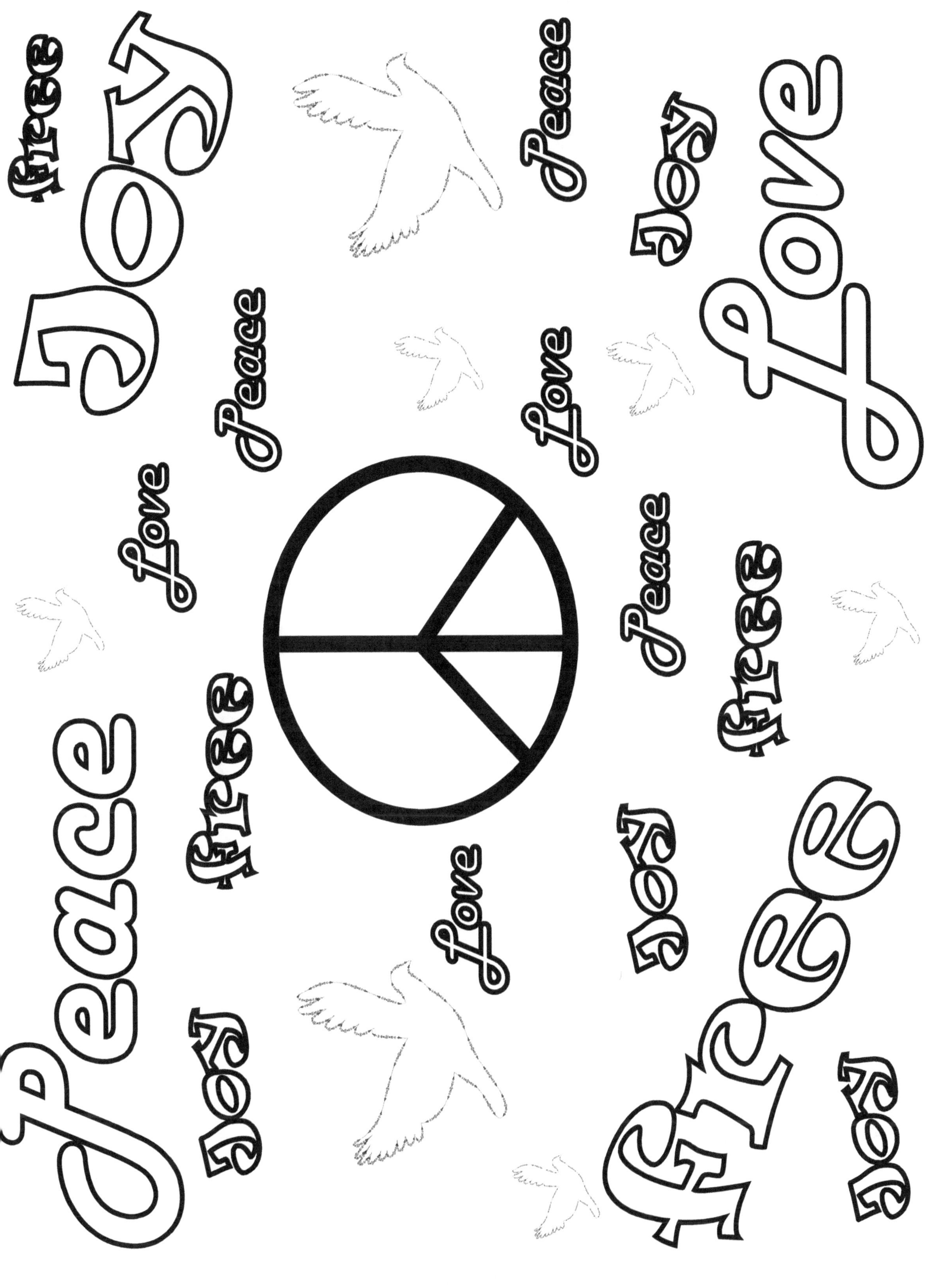

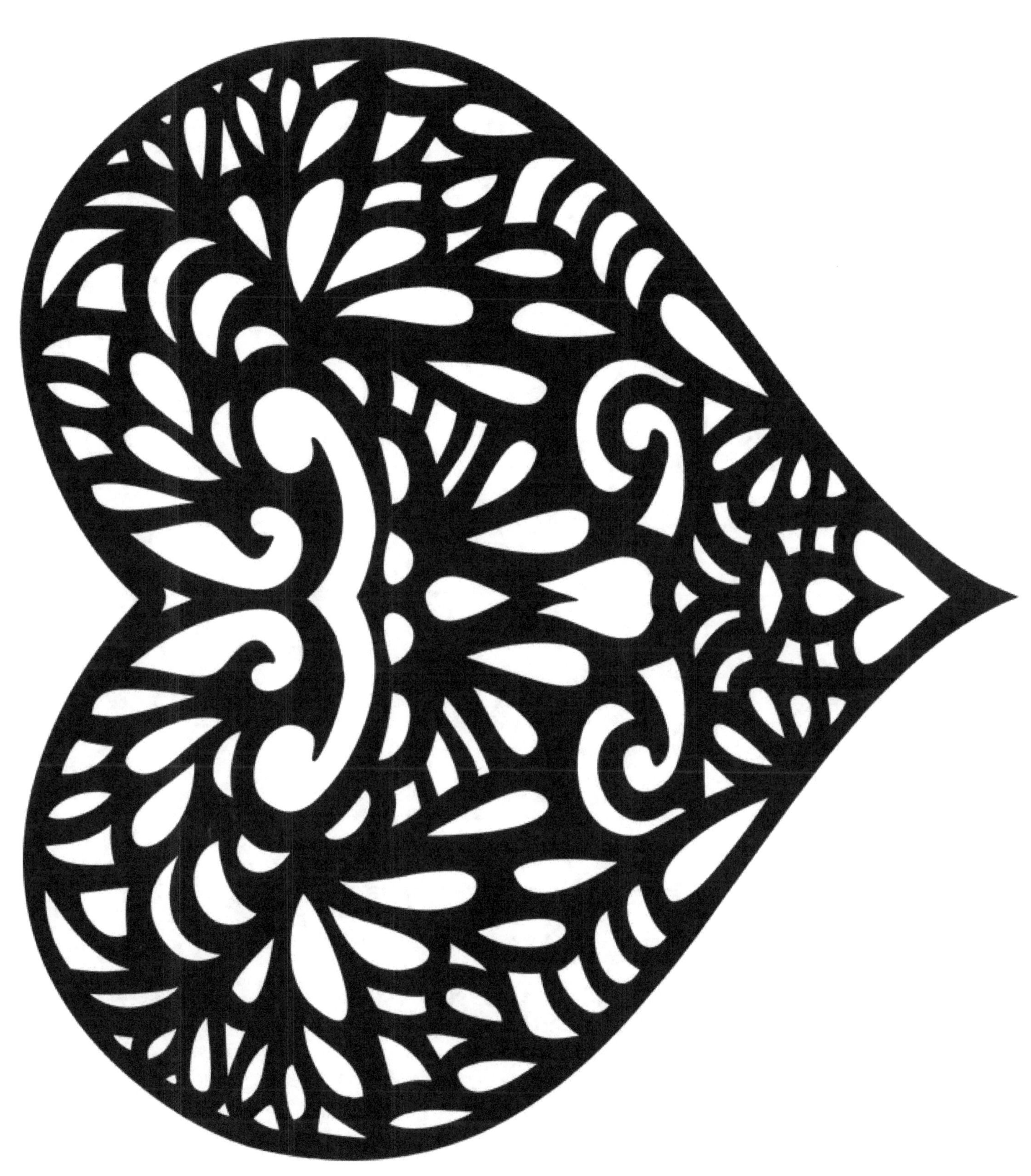

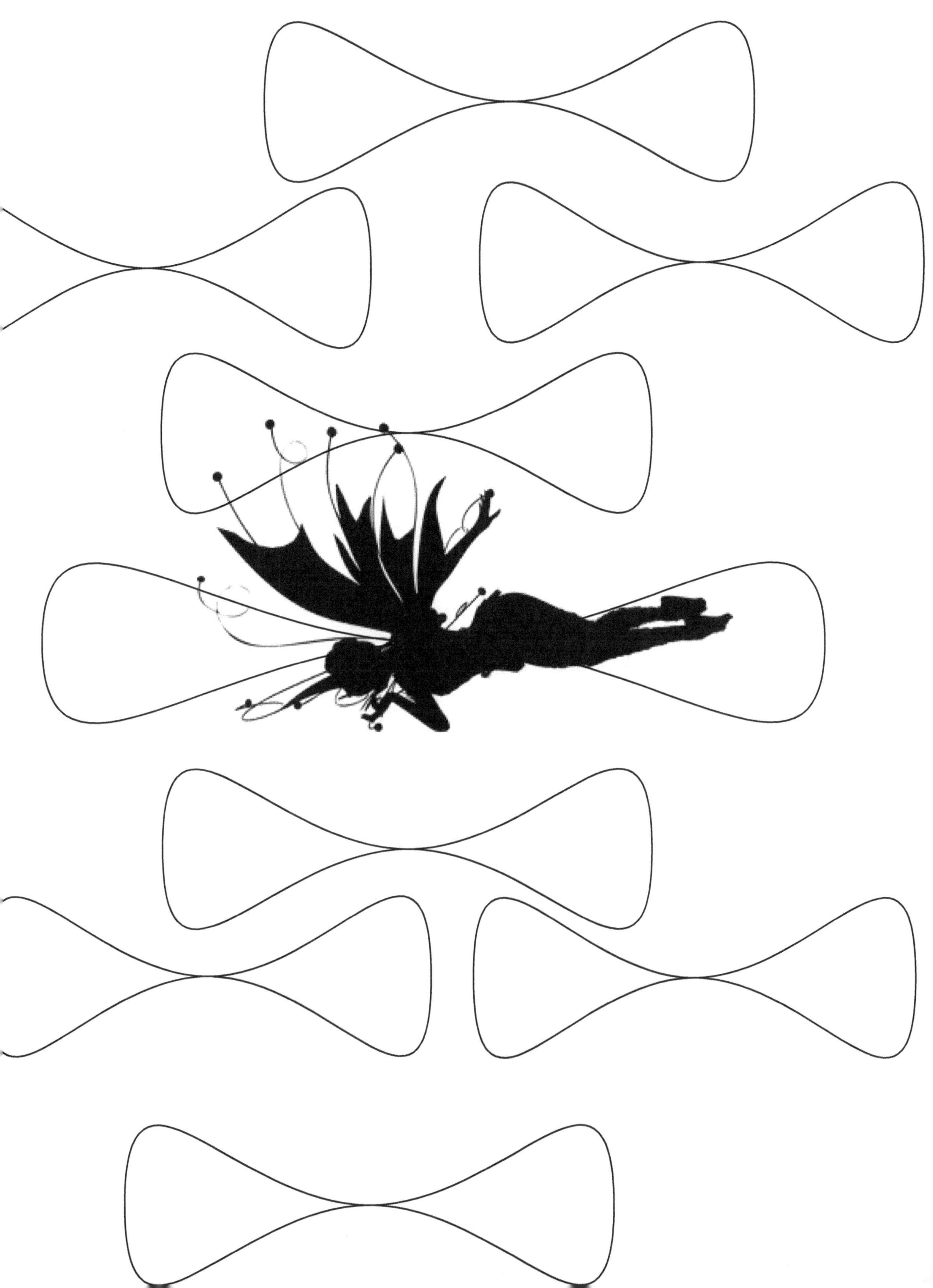

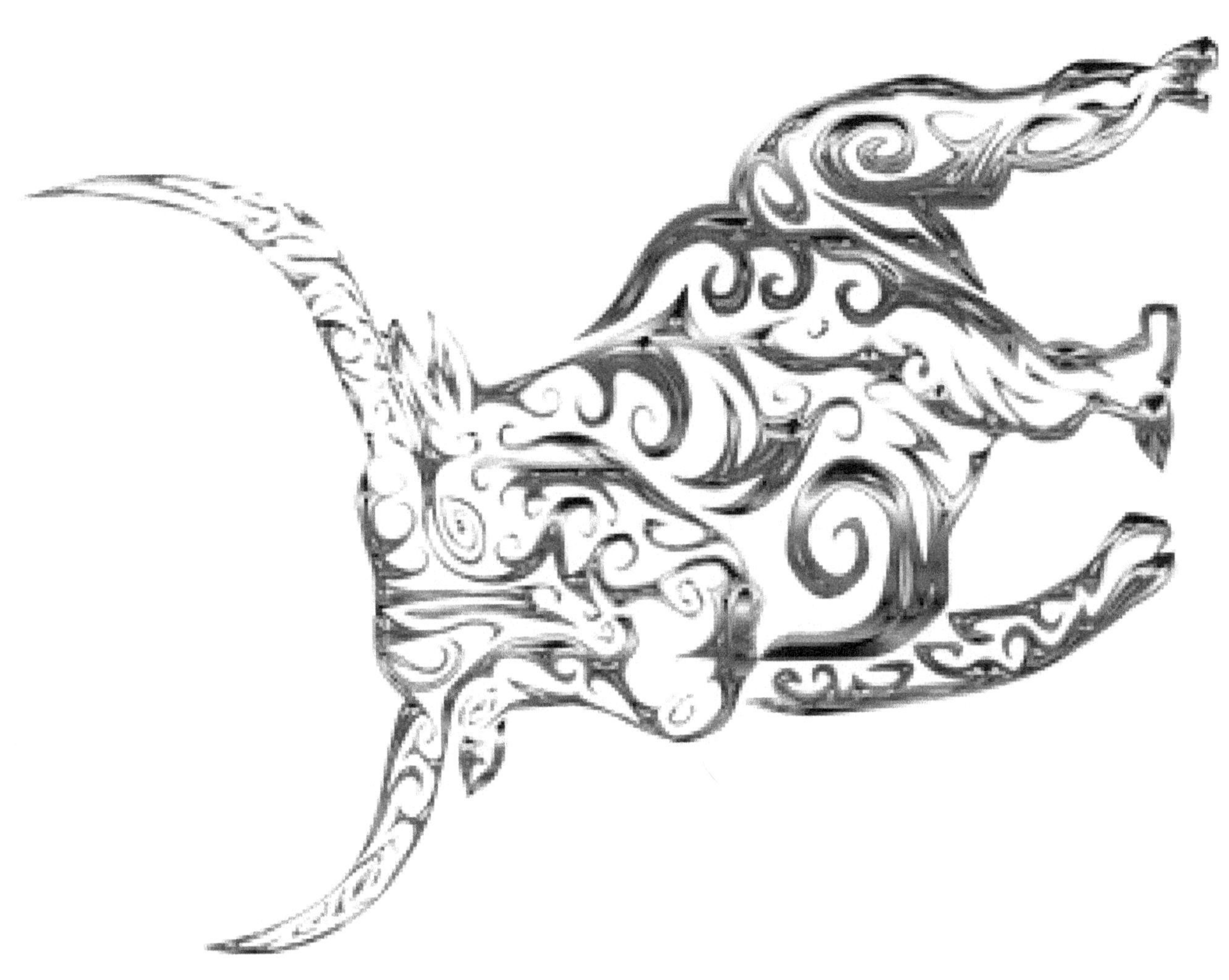

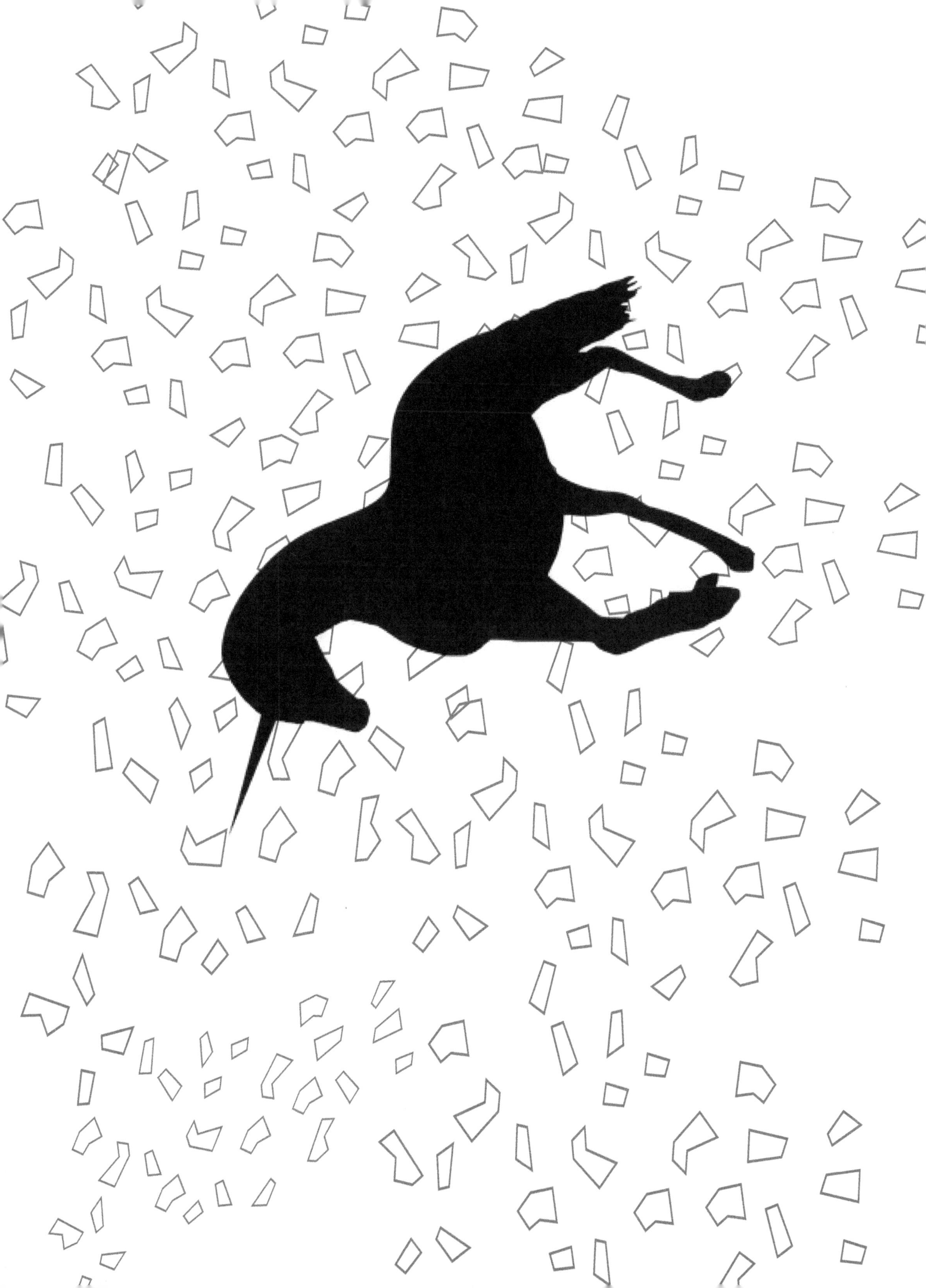

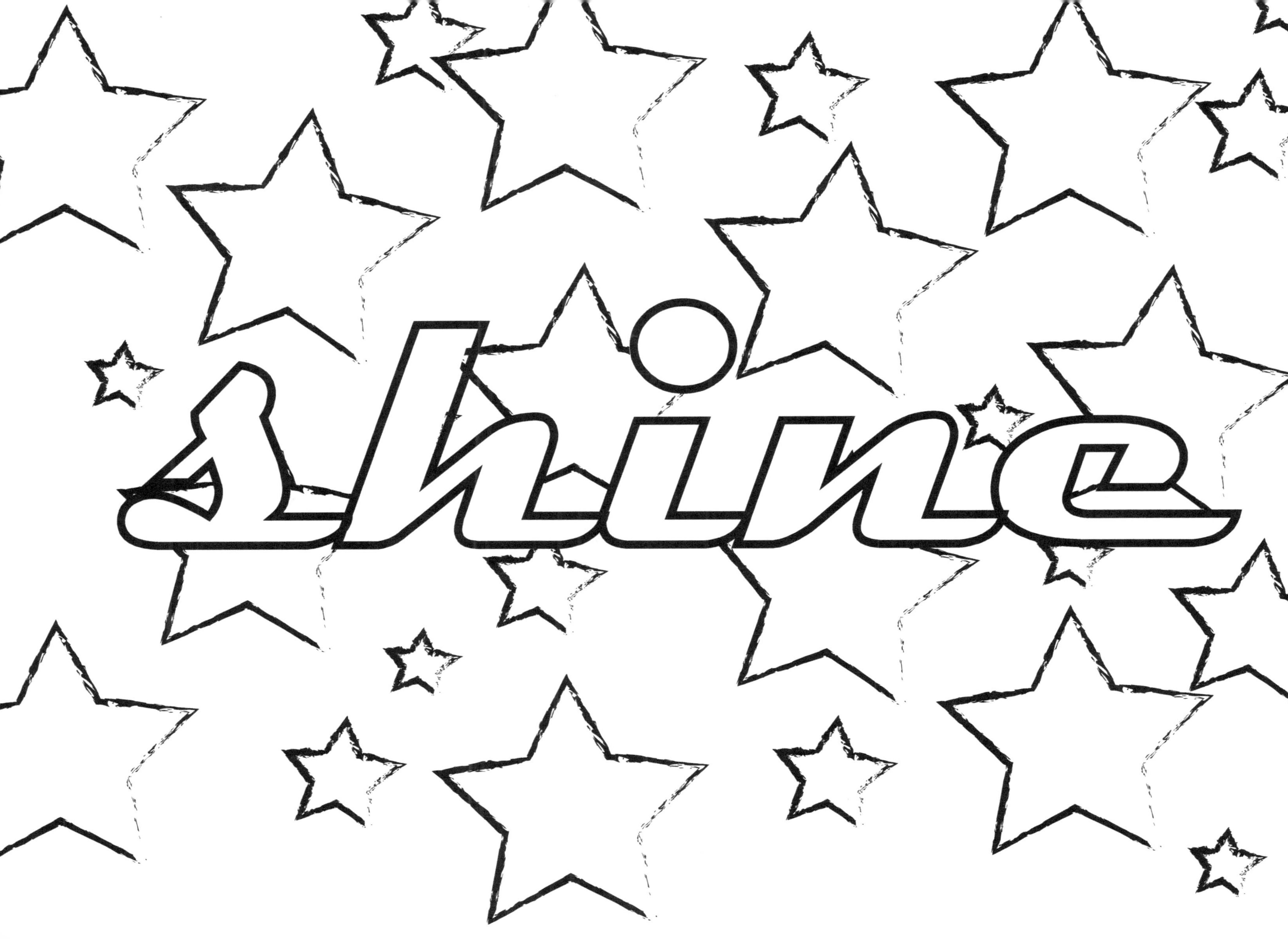

shine

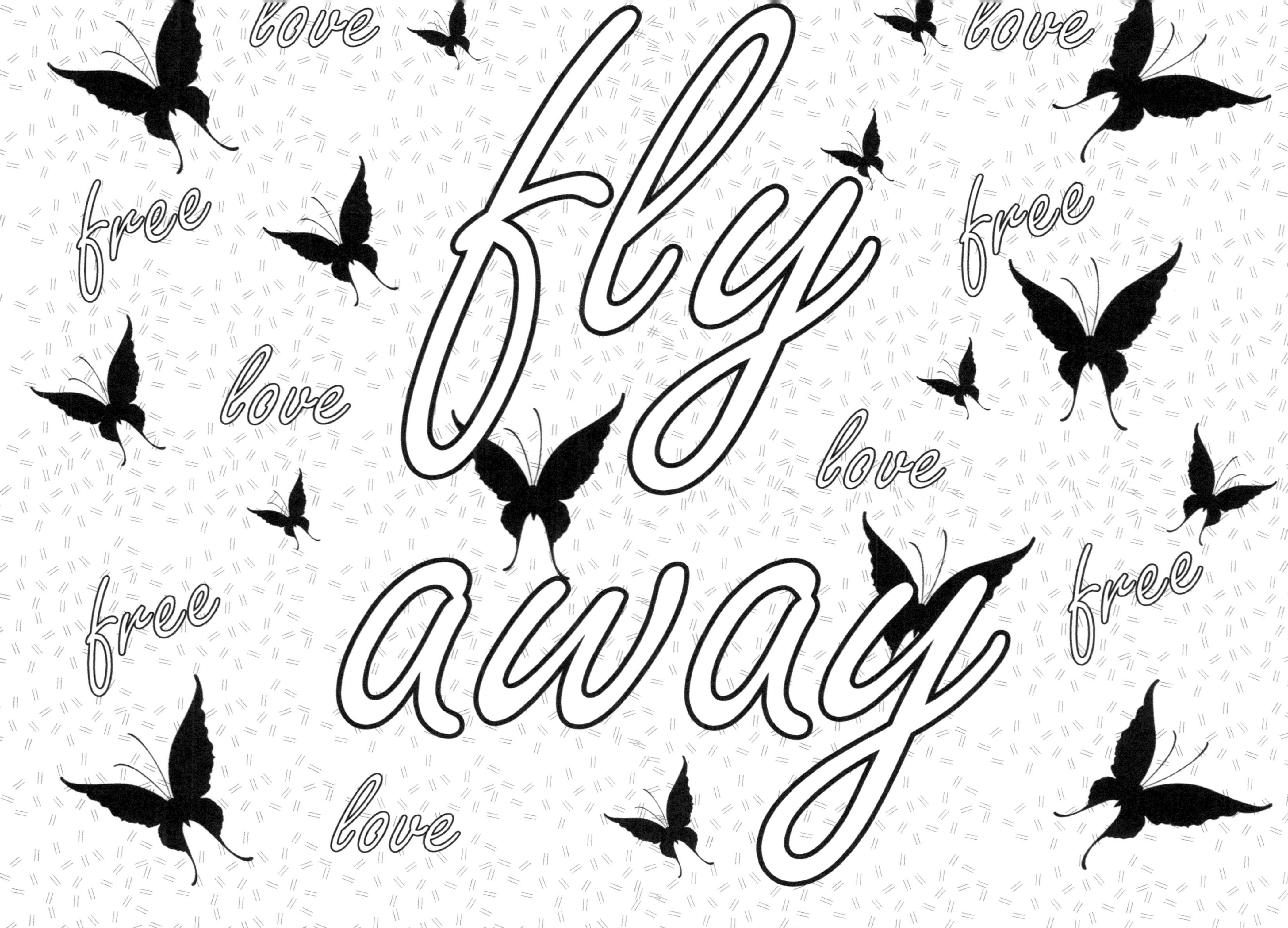

fly away
love
free
love
love
free
free
love
free
love

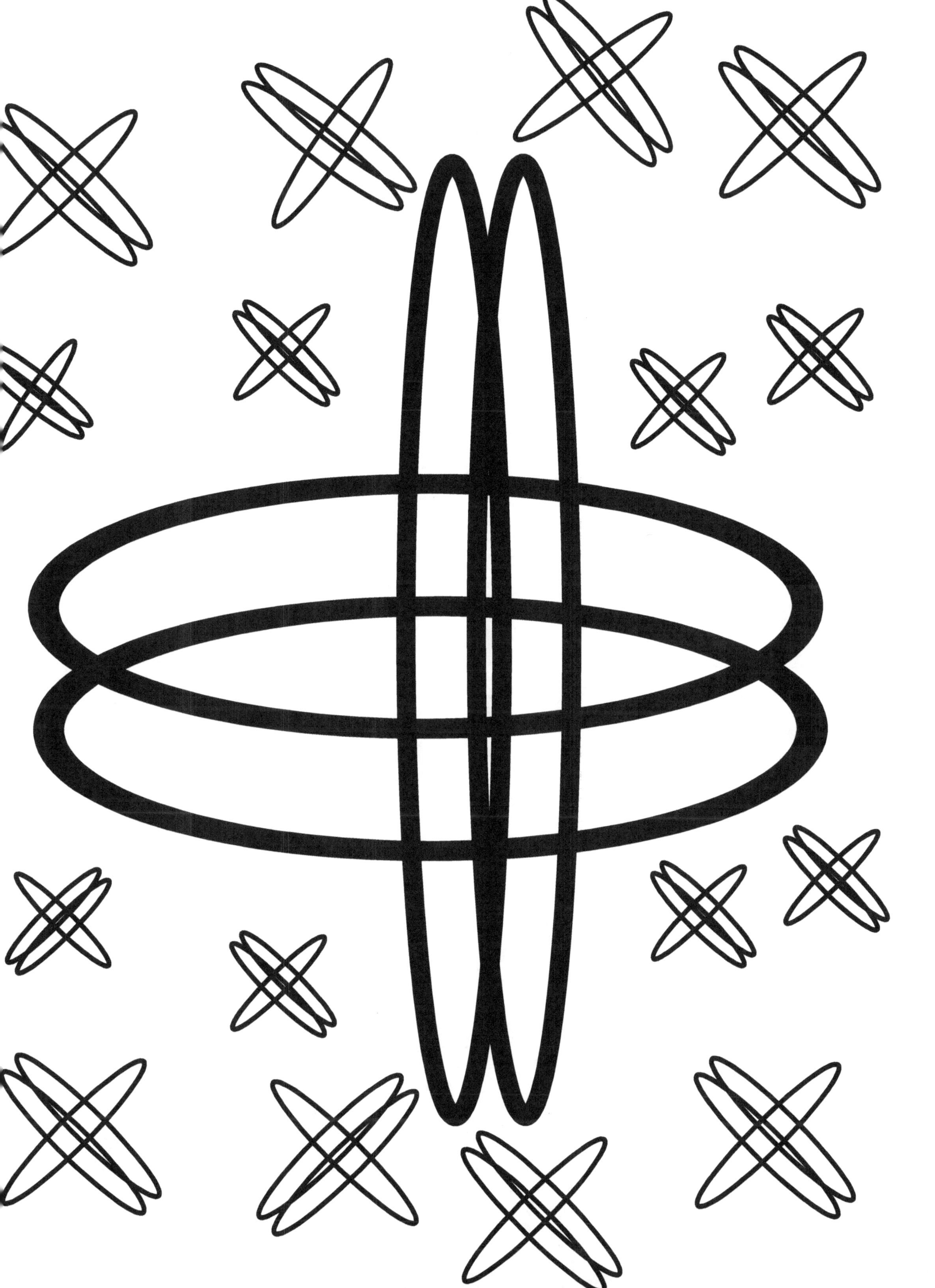

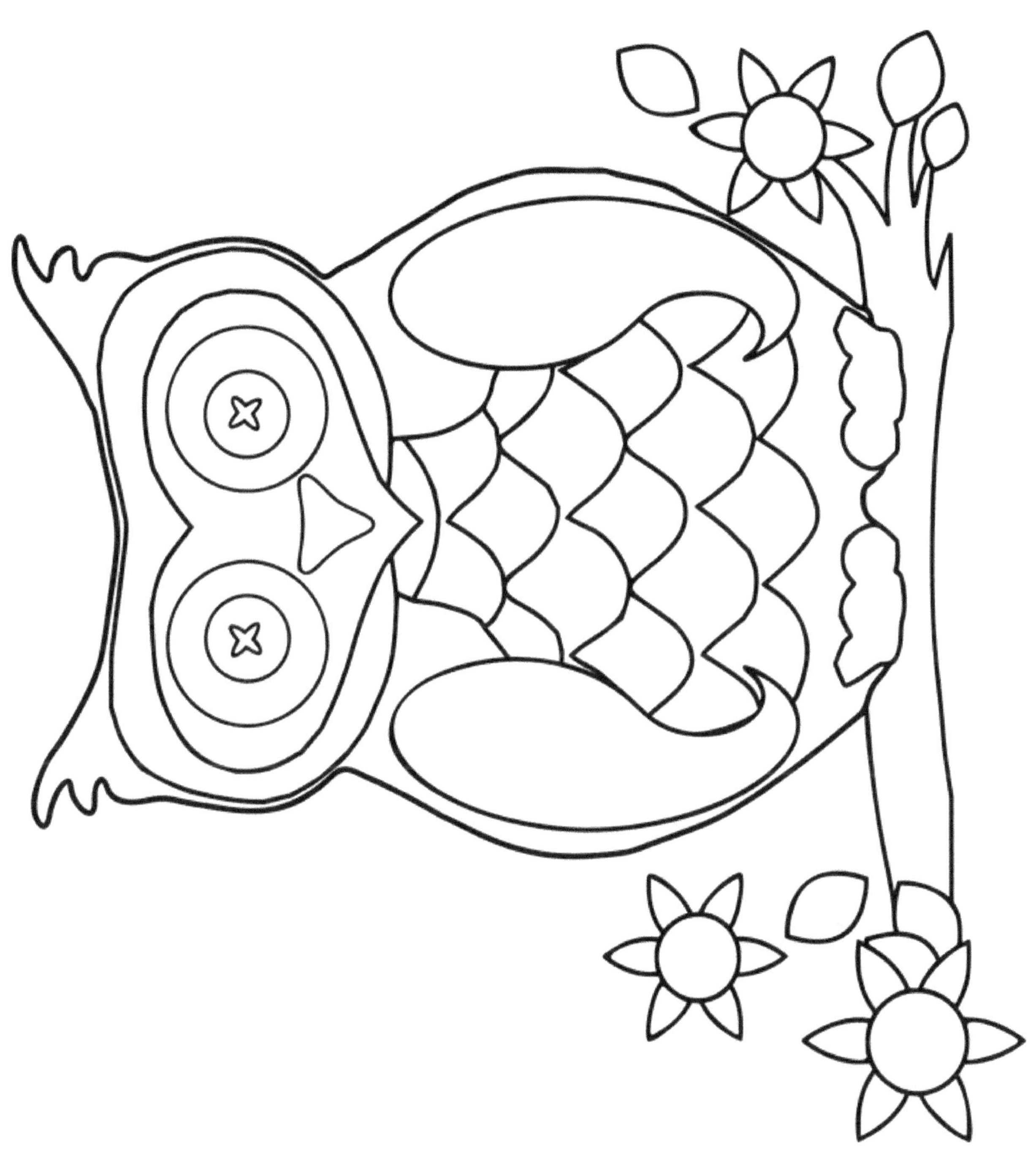

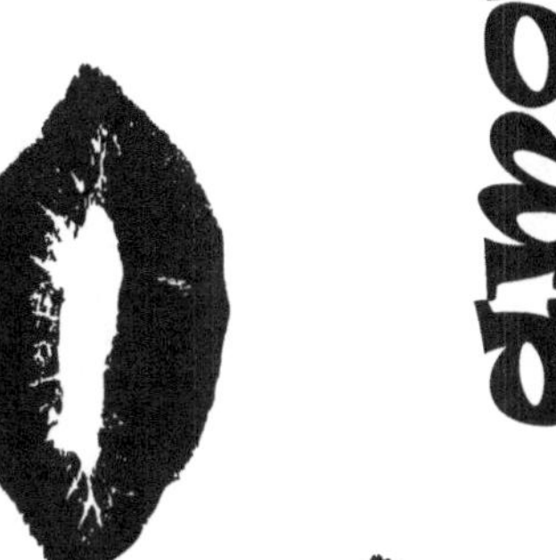
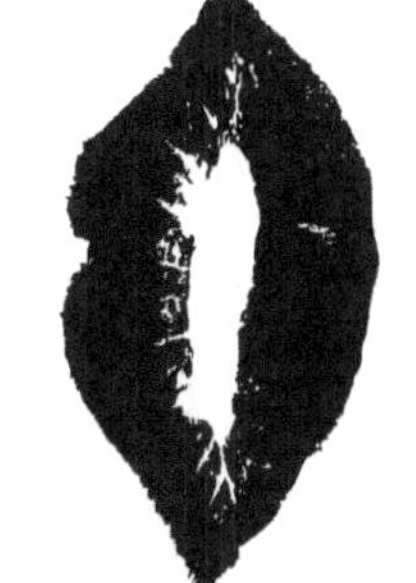
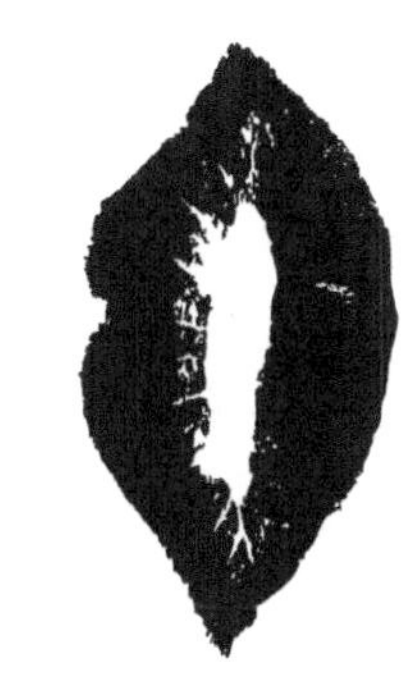
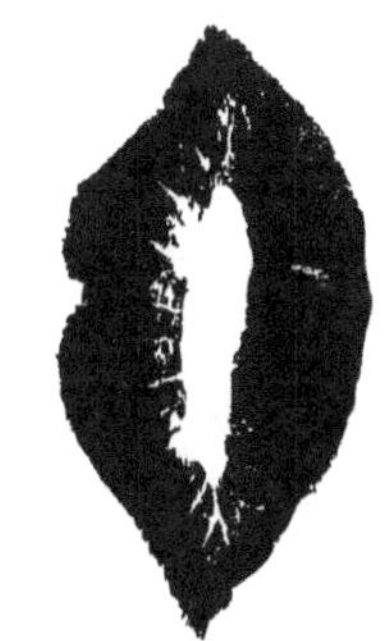
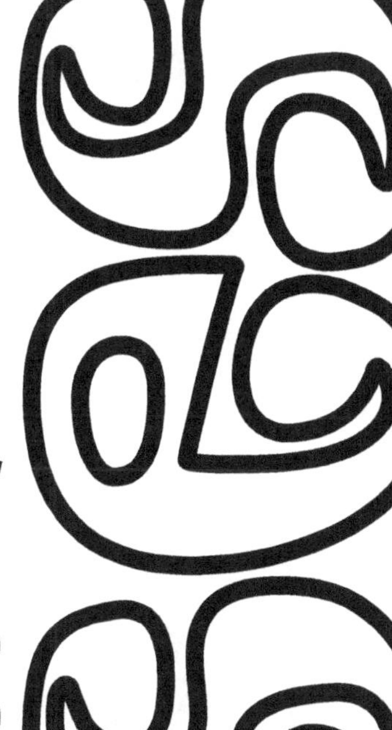
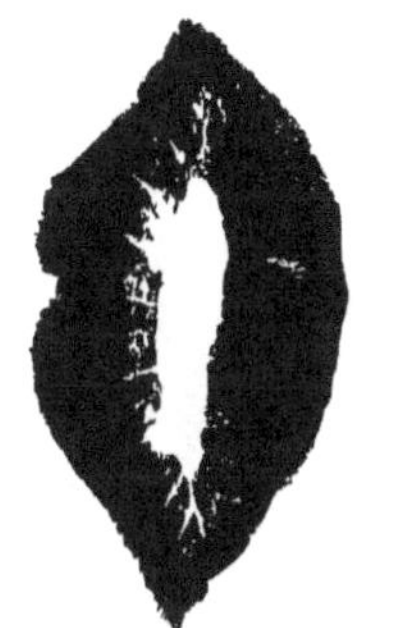
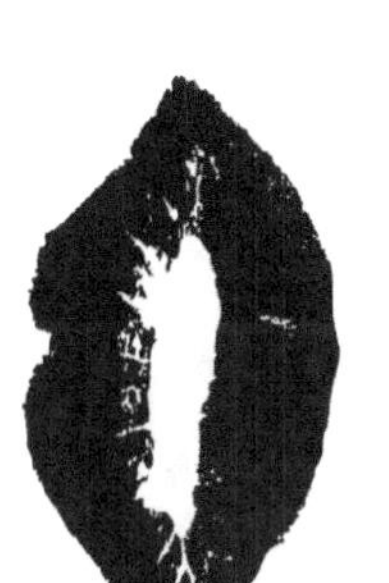
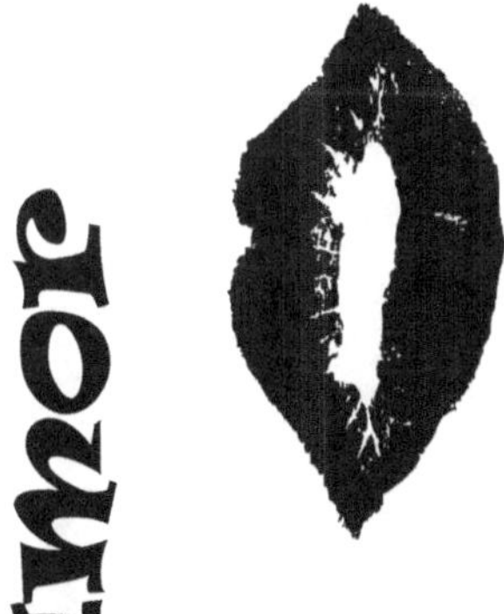
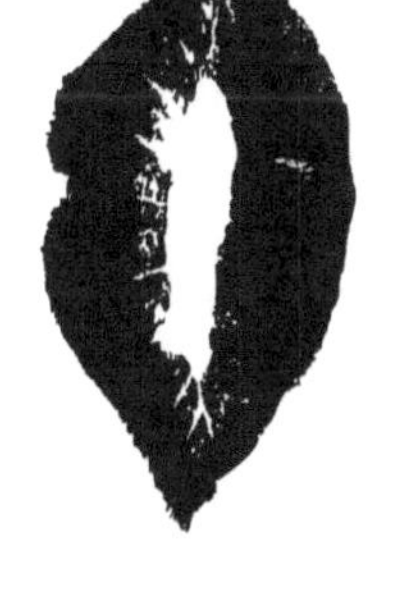

KISSES

hugs
amor
hugs
smooches
amor
smooches
hugs
hugs
smooches
amor
smooches
hugs
amor
smooches
amor
hugs
smooches

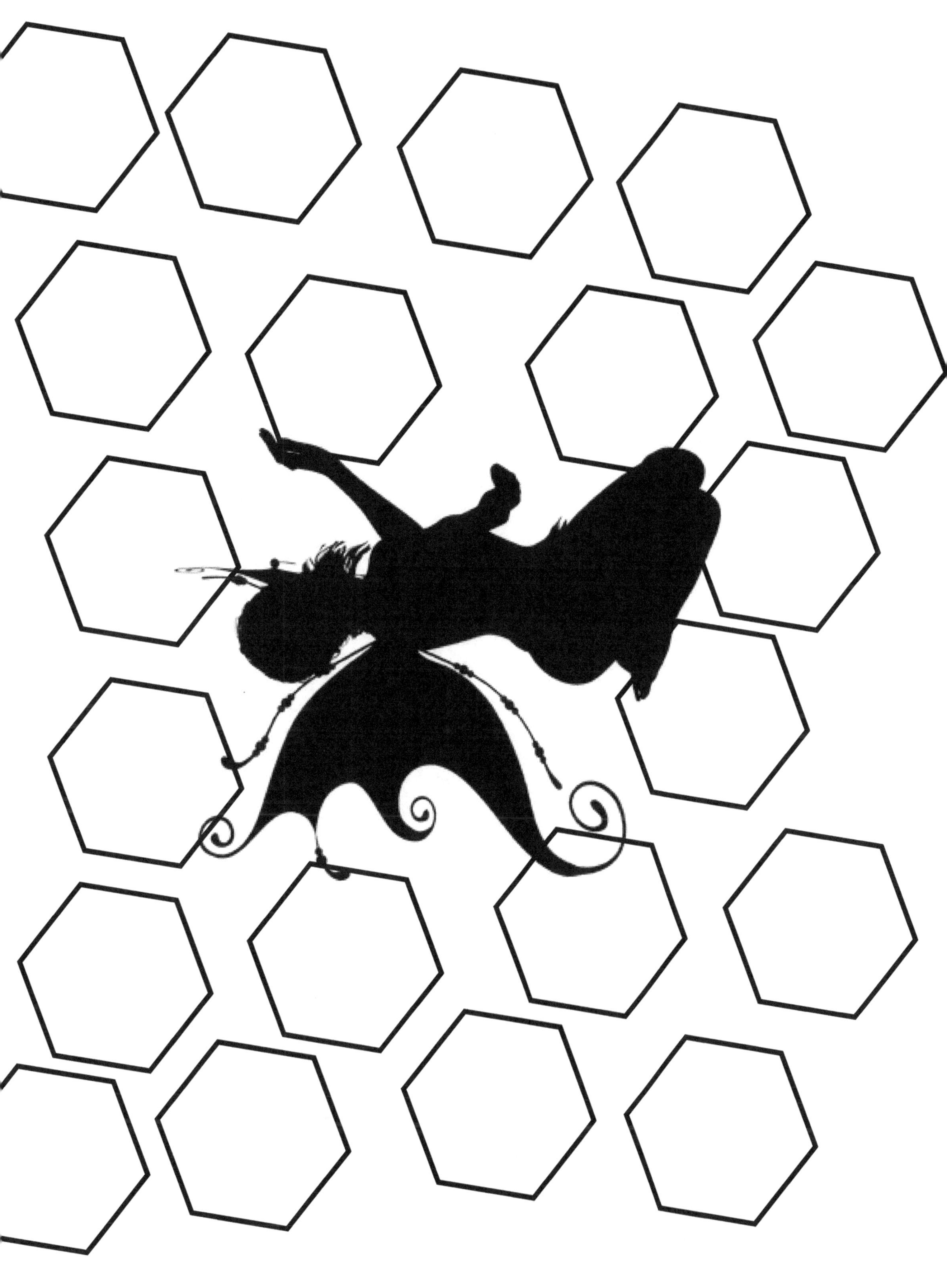

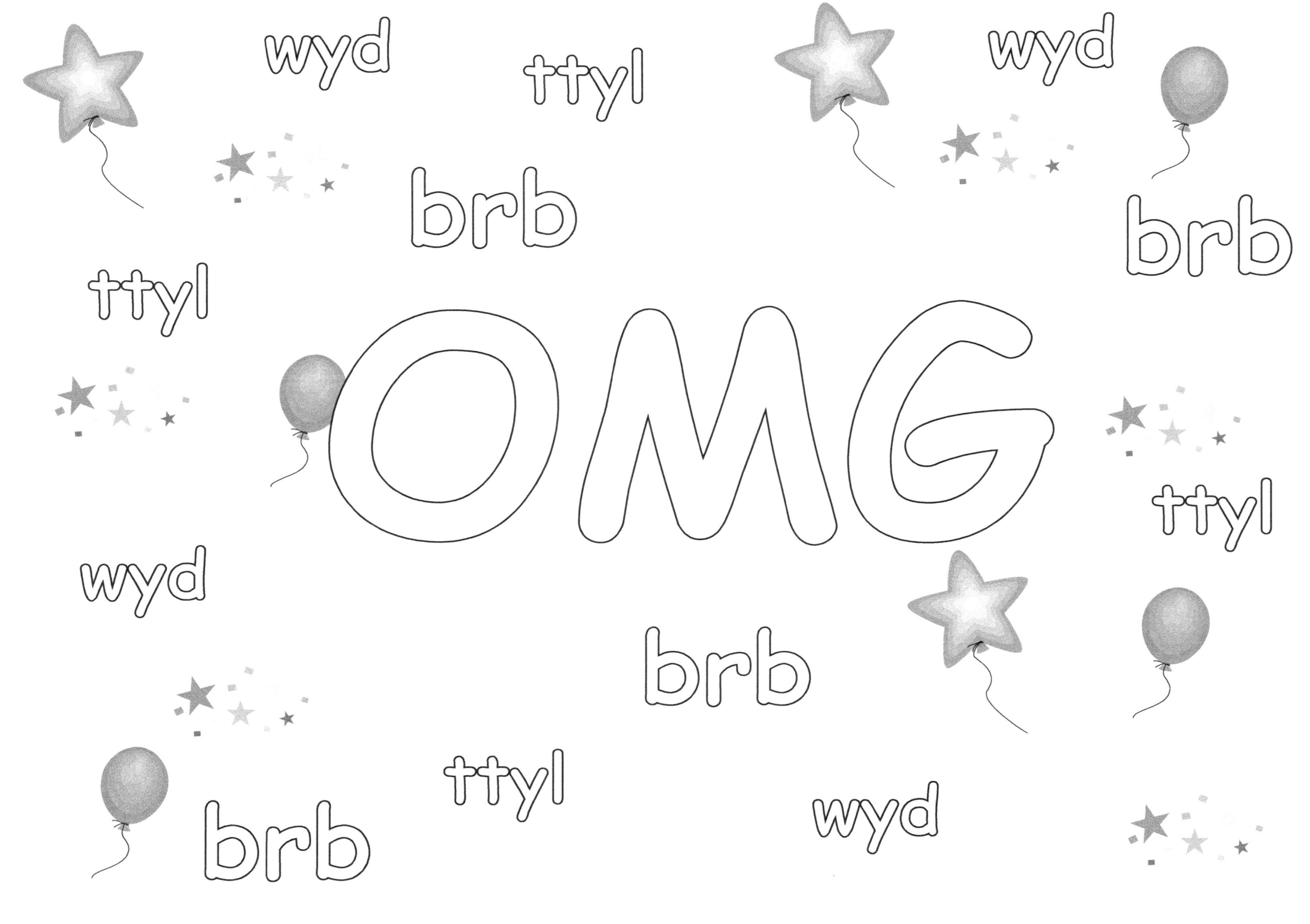

wyd
ttyl
wyd
brb
brb
ttyl
OMG
ttyl
wyd
brb
brb
ttyl
wyd

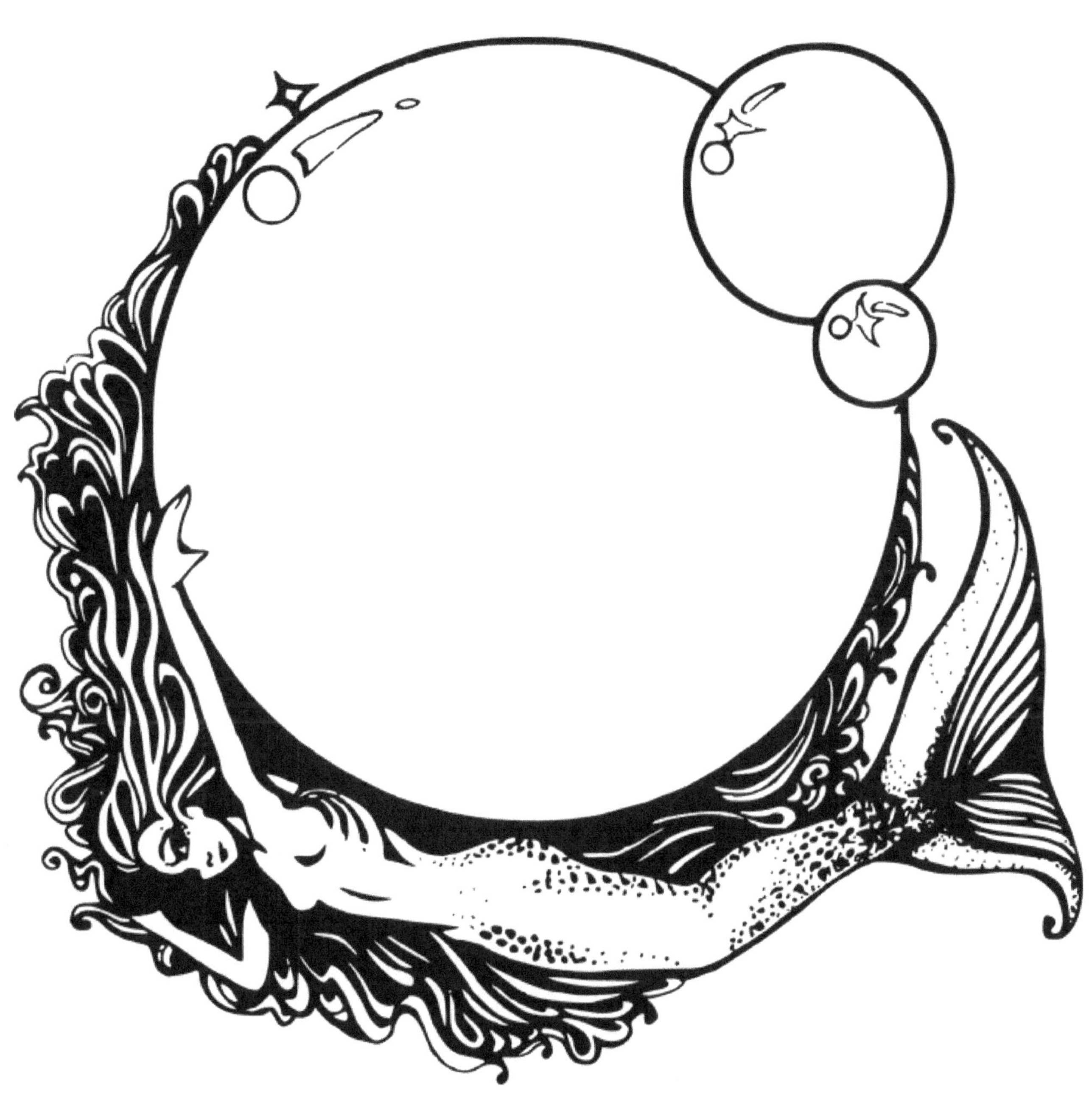

This book belongs to:

Contact info: